Published by Experience Transfer, LLC



ISBN : 978-0-9712883-1-7



Revision History
Rev 1. May 2012
Rev 2. March 2013

# Table of Contents

# Background

This booklet is written for someone who is about to learn or has a working knowledge of Report Studio feels there is much more to learn. It's for beginning through intermediate Report Studio Developers.

This booklet is different than most technology books in that it does not covers how to work the software ... there are no instructions on how to drop items into reports, which properties to change to get which effect or covering the proper syntax . If you have been conditioned into thinking "how to" is all that technology books offer, you are not alone.

It is my experience that books and information like that which is contained within the booklet is fairly rare. I have lived a 30 year life as a PC developer and bought thousands of dollars of technical books, read thousands of web postings, am a very proficient web searcher and am able to digest information fairly quickly. This type of knowledge is fairly rare. You will occasionally find it as an off-hand remark in a technical book, but rarely as its' own paragraph let alone chapter.

I believe that this occurs for four reasons:

1) At the deepest levels of knowledge, any skills become unconscious ... people know what to do but are not really sure exactly why and putting words to the reasons becomes very difficult. See: http://en.wikipedia.org/wiki/Four_stages_of_competence

2) Technical people are generally known for not being able to communicate about technology in non-technical ways and thus create a learning barrier to those without a significant technical understanding and vocabulary. Translating from highly complex into simple is very difficult.

3) Most people cannot summarize knowledge into essential principles or overarching rules.

4) Some people feel that this hard-won knowledge is too valuable to share and would create competition and comparison for themselves.

This booklet will however teach you some of the more difficult things to learn about Report Studio. The underlying rules or principles that are often not conveyed by traditional books and training. The art of using Report Studio as contrasted to the technique.

For illustration of what this booklet is, we are referring to the difference between knowing how to use a word processing program, and knowing how to write clear, simple sentences into paragraphs and paragraphs into chapters. Learning how to work the word processor takes a few weeks. Learning to write clearly and simply takes years.

This booklet hopes to accelerate your experience by many months and to help you become an advanced developer in ½ the time. Read the information and observe it in action as you develop reports. When you get stuck on developing a report, come here and reread the sections and it may trigger ideas. Eventually, this knowledge will become part of you and sink into the unconscious and guide your work in an ongoing way. It is my sincere hope that I can help you get there significantly faster than you normally would have.

Let me know where I succeed and fail. I'm a Kaizen writer.

Ray Hogan

Branchburg, NJ

# It's All About the Query

Creating an advanced report with Report Studio is usually more about creating the query than it is about the formatting and presentation of the data.

There are two fundamental limitations in Report Studio that cause you to become very proficient in creating more complex queries. The first is that a query result set is affected by the filters that operate on it, and, if you need to report two different subsets of data (meaning that the filter conditions are different), you can't do that within one query.  This is traditionally done using multiple queries and joining or unioning them together. In order to become a more advanced report developer, you should become proficient in using joins and unions.

The second limitation in Report Studio is that a report frame (a list, crosstab, chart, repeater, etc.) can only draw its data from one query. There is only a single Query Property of a report frame and that frame must pull all of its data from that query.

This combination of limits suggests that in order to make more complex reports, the report developer must concoct a strategy of queries, unions, calculations and filters that push, shove and otherwise get the data into one, final query so it can be attached to a report frame , and rendered into a usable report.

Indeed, in practice this is exactly the skill you need in order to become an advanced report developer.

## Example #1 Unions:

Imagine you have a requirement to show the number of new registrants to a website in a report. On the first line of a list report you have to show the number of registrants last week, and on the second line, the number last month.

| Registrants | Count |
|---|---|
| Last Week | 25 |
| Last Month | 189 |

Because you have two sets of data needing different filters, you would need to have one query for each time frame and then union the queries together showing the results in a list report from the final (unioned) query.

Query #1: last week

Query #2: last month

Query #3: Union Container

Example #2 ... Joins:

Say you have a report specification to show the overall number of registrants last month in one column, the dollar amount spent by people who registered last year from Germany in column #2 and the total company sales last year in column three.

| Overall Reg. Last Month | Last Month $$ Spend LY – Reg in Germany | Total LY $$ Sales |
|---|---|---|
| 453 | $56,828 | $12,846,133 |

Here again, you can't perform this with one query as you have different filter conditions that stop you from using one query for the three different sets of data you seek.

In this scenario, you would need a total of five queries. For the actual data, you would make three queries, each with the different measurement and appropriate filters to produce your data. You also need each query to have a key field enabling the join. This key field can be from the table if you have one, or, can be invented as a value using a calculated data item. After you have your "data generating" queries, you then join the three queries into one final query (In pairs) and populate the list report from that query.

So the set of queries would look like this:

Query #1: (number of registrants last month)

Query #2: ($$ spent by Germans last year)

Query #3: (LY Total $$ sales)

Query #4: (Join Query #1 & Query #2)

Query #5: (Join Query #4 & Query #3)

Normally, the first big technical task you will do when taking on a report design is to spend some time devising a query strategy and then build/test the strategy.

Complex reports can have tens of queries or more, so take your time, use good query naming conventions, put the queries in a logical layout (visually) in the query screen and test them individually as you go.

# How to Break Down a Report Requirement into a Query Strategy

What follows is an extremely simple statement that will have a huge impact on your report development. Do not take its length as an indication of its lack of importance. It is among the most powerful ideas in this booklet.

The simplest rule to remember when looking at how you will construct your queries is to look at where the filter conditions need to be different. If you need different filters to operate on different subsets of data, then you need a query for each subset. Once you have your subsets defined, then you can determine how to put the subsets back together with joins and/or unions into one final query.

Remember that Unions are used to "add rows" and Joins are used to "add columns".

This simplified analysis will help you quickly break down even the most complex report requirements and devise a query strategy.

# Summary Functions

One of the most important series of functions you will use in Report Studio are called the summary functions. Summary functions are "group" calculations like total, average, minimum, maximum, standard deviation, count, running-count and others. Summary Functions perform their math on all or subsets of data within your database.

The importance of these functions cannot be understated to report development. The names of the functions are self-describing; however the usefulness is broad and deep in reporting.

There are several forms of the function, but in general, you can perform the function at different "levels" within the report. For example, taking total as an example summary function, you can calculate an overall report total, or, you could create one sub-total per grouped field within the report. If you have different groups, you can choose which group to create the sub totals for. Say you have a report that has Continent, Country, State, County and City and the measure is the population of each City. Using the TOTAL summary function, you could calculate the overall population, the population per Continent, per Country etc. The real key to understanding the usefulness is that you can perform these calculations and have the value available in every corresponding row of data. See the data below to better understand what I mean.

## Example Data

| Continent | Country | State | County | City | Pop | Total County | Total State |
|---|---|---|---|---|---|---|---|
| North America | USA | NJ | Middlesex | City A | 100 | 370 | 900 |
| North America | USA | NJ | Middlesex | CityB | 120 | 370 | 900 |
| North America | USA | NJ | Middlesex | City C | 150 | 370 | 900 |
| North America | USA | NJ | Morris | City D | 170 | 530 | 900 |
| North America | USA | NJ | Morris | City E | 160 | 530 | 900 |
| North America | USA | NJ | Morris | City F | 200 | 530 | 900 |
| North America | USA | PA | Bucks | City Z | 300 | 610 | 1,360 |
| North America | USA | PA | Bucks | City Y | 310 | 610 | 1,360 |
| North America | USA | PA | Delaware | City X | 350 | 750 | 1,360 |
| North America | USA | PA | Delaware | City W | 400 | 750 | 1,360 |

As you can see above, the County total is repeated in each row that is within the same County. The same happens for each State. This is an example of Summary functions in action.

One common use of summary functions is when you need to calculate what percentage the current row is of a larger grouping in the reports. In our example, say you want to know the percentage each City is of its' own County. In this case, you would write a summary function totaling each County, and then add a calculation to determine the current row (City population) as a percentage against its own Counties total. (City X has 10% of County ABC's population)

Above, you will see that the total column for County is totaling all the rows that have the same County as the current record. This would enable you (for example) to then calculation what percentage the current City is of its' own County.

## Another Example of the need for Summary Functions.

Say you have a situation where your database has regularly sampled data; say a reading of the height of gasoline in a storage tank. However the database holds the readings for 100 different tanks and the measurement is made every minute for every tank. Your task is to determine the overall total of all tanks and then plot the hourly value to look for trends when the set of tanks are being changed rapidly. In this case, you will need to calculate the hourly average for each tank (you can't add up the reading every minute as your number would be about 60 times too high), and then calculate the total of the hourly averages across all tanks.

Without using the summary functions, you could average them, or total them but neither would give you the current total. Moreover, you would not be able to plot them in a graph as you need a reading per hour that could then be plotted.

In this case, you would create two summary functions (or one with nested functions if you understand nesting). The first summary function would calculate the hourly average level per tank, the second one would total the hourly averages per hour. You would chart the results of the second summary function.

## How to write summary functions

Here is the basic form... I'll use "total" but the same syntax applies for count, min, max, etc.

total( [measurement] for [group level1],[grouplevel2])

Here I am not using the standard form of parenthesis and brackets but only communicating the idea. Things inside of square brackets are Report Studio Fields (A.K.A. query subjects).

Here's a breakdown:

"Total" is the name of the summary function you want (Your options can be found in the summaries folder under the functions tab of the calculation window (double click a column in your report frame, or add a calculation to a report)

[measurement] is the field you want to perform the function on... it will typically be a numeric field for total, average etc., but if you are counting things, it can be a text field.

"for"

Literally you enter the word "for". This part of the function is the most important to understand. I advise people to translate the word for to: "at the following level in the report", or "for each individual combination of". You still have to write "for" but you can think the longer phrases above in order to reinforce your thinking as you construct the calculation.

[group level 1 ], etc.

Here you list each group level you want the function calculated for. So in our case above, if you want to calculate the average for each hour for each tank, you would have in the "for" list: [tank], [hour]. You can use the fields from the package or from the query tab in the insertable objects panel.

So to read the whole function in human understandable narrative, "calculate the average of the gasoline level for each unique combination of tank and hour."

## Be Very Careful with Understanding Your Data

One crucial thing to understand is that you need to be specific on your list of levels. If there is a condition in your data where the values could be similar for different sub groups AND you have not been specific, the calculation will combine multiple values from different groups and give you an incorrect value, but only where there are duplicates. The intermittent nature of this error will make it more difficult to detect. Be explicit in your list of field and you will be protected from this sneaky report bug.

**Example for being specific with your "for" values in Summary Functions:**

In our earlier data we had Continent, Country, County, City.

If you were calculating the total for each County and you wrote:

total([population] for [county]), you have just created a error because (at least in the USA) there are similarly named Counties in different States, the query that will be run will combine ALL data from ANY county with the same name, even if it is in a different state.

The proper form is:

```
total( [population] for [continent],[country],[state],[county] )
```

Read this as "calculate the total for each unique combination of Continent, Country, State and County".

If instead, you got lazy and just listed state and county, you are at risk of there being two different countries which have the same state or province names and within it the same county. It's probably unlikely, but unless you are a geography master, you can't be sure... In my experience, you will be much happier if you just take the safe route and list the entire hierarchy and totally eliminate any risk of unintended combination now and in the future.

In the USA, there are 31 counties named "Washington". There are 28 cities named Springfield in the USA. What is the chance that two different Springfields are in Washington County in two different States? Save yourself time and frustration by being explicit.

# Avoid Master-Detail Whenever Possible

In technology, there are often things that are good in theory and not as good, or even a bad idea in practice. Master-detail reports are one such thing.

A master-detail report is, on paper a great mechanism. Imagine a scenario where you need to make a series of charts for individual group values. How can you do it in Report Studio?

A master-detail report starts with a list report containing the grouped value, then, you add a chart into the body of the list. (Other report frames can be added into the list too).

For example, imagine you need to create a bar chart for each State in the USA. You would start with a list report that contains State, then add into the list body (with the insert cursor showing) a chart from the toolbox and populate the series, measure etc. of the chart.

If you take a look at your queries at this point you will see that there are two queries, one attached to the list and one attached to the chart.

The last step in setting up a master detail report is to relate the two queries. To do this you need to add the common field between the two queries, in this case State. You can add State to the chart query directly. Then you would establish the master-detail relationship between the queries from the Data/Master-detail Relationships menu. You establish the master-detail relationship by first selecting on the part of the report that is the detail. If you then right click the selected report frame, you should see "master detail relationships" in the context menu.

When you run the report, you would find that you now have a bar chart, for each State where the data in the bar is filtered to show only the current States' values.

It's a very slick and powerful capability.

## What's the problem with Master-Detail Reports?

The downside in Report Studio is that each time a chart is rendered, the reporting engine runs a separate query for each State. This implies that 51 Queries would need to be run... one query for the list and one for each State.

This is where the performance hit occurs.

It depends on the speed of your inner query and the number of times you iterate from the outer, State query, but overall report performance can quickly become very slow.

## What to do if you must use a Master-Detail:

Spend significant time improving the efficiency of the inner (detail) query. Use key fields in the join when possible, find out if there are any indexes on the fields/tables used in the inner query and if possible use filters on those fields, remove unneeded fields and remove calculations if possible. Another big thing is to look deeper into the model to find out if any of the fields you use in the detail query are themselves from another table and see if you can add them to a new query and then join that query in later.

## Alternatives to Master-Detail Reports

Unfortunately, the example above may be difficult to solve without using a Master-Detail. One idea that is slightly painful is to create one bar chart with a prompt on state and then create 49 report views of that report. It's administratively grueling but it gets rid of the master detail. Another is to look into bursting the report with the burst key on state. If you inner frame happens to be a list, you can use grouping and page breaks to accomplish what you want.

If you have a situation where you have only a few rows in the outer query, then a master detail is usually OK, but when you have hundreds or thousands or rows, master-detail reports will quickly bog down and has the potential to be amongst the worst performing reports you make.

# Use Indexed Fields in Filters for Increased Performance

As a report developer, you need to understand some crucial concepts from database technology in order to increase the performance of your reports.

The top of the list is Table Indexes and Key Fields.

In database technology, an index is a speed enhancing technique were, in effect, the database keeps a table of contents of the database on specific fields in order to speed up the access to data within the table. The fields that are used are determined by the database designer or DBA. This technique, called indexing is done with one or more fields in a given table and can give incredible speed improvements, but only when using the same field(s) that exist in the index.

As a report developer, and although it may not be a direct requirement of your job, you should always have a good idea of which fields in the database are indexed and you should always be on the lookout to use them in filter situations in order to benefit from indexing technology.

## How to Use an Index

To use an index, all you need to do is to use the field on which the index is made within in a filter expression, and, ideally use it alone.

For example, say you have a field called "State_Name" and you also have one called "State_ID" (The unique number representing the State).

A brief discussion with your DBA or database designer may reveal that the State_ID field is the field on which the indexing was performed. Imagine you are working on a report that needs to list all of the sales in NY. You could use either the State_Name or the State_ID field in your filter. Using the State ID field makes your report less understandable, but using State_Name makes it slower. The best trade-off in this scenario is to use the State_ID and add a comment into your filter for clarity and future understanding.

## Using Key Fields in Prompts

When making prompts that present choices to the user, you will have a choice of which fields to use for the prompt. However, you will now have a different problem. The user of your report will want to see values that they understand but you want to use the Indexed Field for performance. Report Studio has a solution.

In a prompt, you can specify both a Use and a Display value... they are two properties of a prompt. FYI "Use" means "use in the filter". When using the prompt wizard, you can set a different Use and Display value and the wizard will take care of the details as well as add the fields to your prompt query. If you need to retrofit the filter, you can later set the Use value property, but you will probably need to modify your prompt query to include the indexed field so you can then select it when setting the Use property in the prompt.

# The Properties Property

In Report Studio, there is a property that you need to know about. This property has the worst name of a property ever, and not knowing about it will occasionally lead you to much frustration and lost time. This property has the unfortunate name of "properties".

That's right, it is called the properties property.

The properties property is not a property of every object in Report Studio; it is a property of a page and a list but notably not a crosstab. It is also the property of a prompt.

Note: If the discussion that follows is foreign to you, just understand that there is a deficiency in Cognos in relation to it "knowing" which fields it needs to perform its function.

The properties property is a "break in case of emergency" type of tool. Sometimes Report Studio is not able to access all field values in your query that it needs to properly create a report. In a case where you seem to have done everything correctly and Report Studio is still not doing what you intend, look to the properties property. The properties property tells Report Studio to look in an additional place other than the ones it usually looks to solve its report rendering challenge.

In Report Studio, one of the properties of a list is the query that it is attached to. Another non visible part is the list of columns that the list pulls from that query for display. When in the execution of a report, it comes time for rendering, the Cognos reporting engine provides only the data needed by the list into the list object. Specifically only those columns that have been included in the report frame design are provided. It does not include other columns that may be in the query.

A gap is caused when you need the data from another query column for sorting or another non-display purpose. For some reason, Cognos does not include the additional columns into the frame and some operations will fail.

The properties property is a way for Report Studio to tell the frame that it also may need access to other columns in the query to perform its function. Specifically you may have a situation where you want to control the sorting order of a list by a field that is not in the list. This is a classical case where you need to set the properties property to include the additional field for sorting. If you had not done so, even though you have indicated which field you would want so sort on, Cognos would neither produce an error, nor, perform the sorting leaving you scratching your head.

In earlier versions of Report Studio, the need to tell the frame about additional fields via the properties property was more important, and in more recent versions they seem to have tightened up the access to the data from the query so you no longer need the set them.

However there are still places in Report Studio where you need to know about the properties property. The most common place is when you need to use a field in a conditional expression that is not rendered into a frame. The expression may not know about the field unless you tell it about it. The symptom here is that you do your entire conditional configuration as needed, and then it does not work and does not throw an error. The simple solution (if you know about it) is to change the properties property of the page to include the field that you are referring to in the condition.

The properties property is one of those mysterious properties that only through much heartache and anguish do developers come to know about.

# Using Logic Within Column Calculations

One powerful technique to use in creating desired values within a query is the "in-column filter".

To understand this, let's ...

## Review aggregation in Cognos.

Recall that Cognos aggregates by default, so it takes all of the values within a numeric column in a table and adds-up (or min or max or average) the values for each unique combination of data values of the non-numeric fields in the query. Then it shows a rolled-up value on each row of the report.

For example, if you have country, state and population in your report. Cognos will show each combination of country/state along with the total population of each pair. In this scenario, the actual database table may hold the population per city, so Cognos will roll up the population of hundreds of cities within a state but upon rendering the report, will show only one row containing the total for the Country/State combinations.

The technique of using in-column filters uses a logical expression in the data item definition to be aggregated. Using this approach, you selectively "bring forward" values from individual rows, so that Cognos can aggregate them. Using the above example, let's say you only want the state total of the cities which have a population under 5,000 ... a "how many people live in small towns by state" report. In this case, you write an IF statement in the population column. The IF checks the current rows' (city's) population and if it is less than 5,000 then the population value of the current row will be used for the column, but if not, then the value will be set to 0.

So your data items code will look something like this.

```
if ([population]<5000) then ([population]) else (0)
```

Taking a moment to think about what the result set will look like (If you turned off auto aggregation), there would be thousands of rows, but all population fields would be 0 unless the value of the population was less than 5,000; then you would see the actual population value. If a given state had multiple cities with populations less than 5,000 you would see records indicating each ones' population value. When Cognos rolled up those values, you would get the grand total of only small cities' population into the rolled up total.

| Continent | Country | State | County | City | Pop | In Column Filter |
|---|---|---|---|---|---|---|
| North America | USA | NJ | Middlesex | City G | 1,000 | 1,000 |
| North America | USA | NJ | Middlesex | City H | 370 | 370 |
| North America | USA | NJ | Middlesex | City I | 12,000 | 0 |
| North America | USA | NJ | Morris | City J | 1,700 | 1,700 |
| North America | USA | NJ | Morris | City K | 1,600 | 1,600 |
| North America | USA | NJ | Morris | City L | 20,000 | 0 |
| North America | USA | PA | Bucks | City S | 30,000 | 0 |

| | | | | | | |
|---|---|---|---|---|---|---|
| North America | USA | PA | Bucks | City T | 31,000 | 0 |
| North America | USA | PA | Delaware | City U | 2,350 | 2,350 |
| North America | USA | PA | Delaware | City V | 3,400 | 3,400 |

In effect you are filtering data but doing so in a calculation instead of a filter.

Alternatively, you could solve the problem using another query with a filter on it for only cities with population less than 5,000 and then joining that column back into the main query joining on state name.

## Other Uses of In-Column Filters

This technique can be used sometimes instead of a join. If you had a report specification where one column needed the state total population of cities that have less than 50,000 population, a second column where the population is between 50,000 and 500,000 and a third where the population is over 500,000 this technique would do the trick. You would merely create 3 data items each with the different threshold logic and then let Cognos roll up the totals.

This technique can also be used as a smart count where you could place a 1 in a column if complex logical conditions are met and 0 if not, and the totaling the column. Cognos will then total the 1's and in effect count the matches.

This technique can also be used to allow you to keep/drop records via a join by modifying or corrupting a key value based on logical conditions. Once you change the key field via calculation, it will no longer find a match in another query and be dropped from your result.

# Use Good Naming and Comments

Report Studio comes up a bit deficient in terms of internal report documentation. For instance commenting things is very non obvious. You can't enter comments about your overall report strategy, change notes etc. Some people will enter them in a hidden page with text items, and that works if not a bit indirect and klugy.   You also cannot name filters. So you will be well served by using strong naming conventions and making sure to stick a name on everything that needs clarification on.

As a practical rule, I tend to name things that you know you will struggle to identify later. I generally do not name things like text fields as you know what they are by reading the text you have specified within them. However functional things like queries, parameters, and filters should always be given names to help others or yourself determine what you were intending to achieve with a particular component.

You can name queries, data items, conditional variables, prompts, pages, lists, crosstabs, charts and a few other things in Report Studio.

## Naming Queries

In moderately complex report designs, queries are one of the places where you will easily get confused without good names. You should note both the purpose and the function each query plays in your report. Make sure to put the queries into some logical visual order so you can gain additional information based on their position.  For example, if you have two base queries, and then you join them, you may want to list the two base queries above (higher in the screen) and the join result immediately below so you can see the logical flow of the Query strategy.

Here are some ideas for naming Queries. These name prefixes could be the base part of your names with the actual purpose listed after the base.

JoinBase (the core data that will be used in conjunction with one or more lookup queries)

JoinLookup (a query that brings in additional fields)

JoinIntermediate (the result of two other queries, but not the final query and this one will itself be used in another join)

JoinFinal (the final, joined query)

UnionDetail (one of base queries to be unioned)

UnionFinal (the final result of all Unioned Queries)

Prompt (a query used to populate a prompt)

Master (in a master-detail report, the master)

Detail (in a master-detail report, the detail)

## Naming Conditional Variables

As parameters are often referred to either with question marks around them, or they are used within a function indicating that they are parameters, you can generally not indicate that a parameter is a parameter as it won't easily be confused with something else. However using a good name for the variables can help others understand your intended use

## Naming Conditional Variable Values

When you configure string variables in Report Studio, you have to devise values that will be generated by the calculation and then you have to create a list of outcomes for the calculation. These outcomes are later used to manipulate the report conditionally through the last step of the conditional reporting configuration process. I recommend naming the values to represent what they will do. For example, if you intend to change part of your report red based on a large number, in your conditional expression and in the outcome, you should use the word “Red”. This will make your job of configuring the conditional report changes much easier as you won’t have to switch back and forth to the variable expression writer to translate what outcome you intended into what color to make it. In effect you are making it self-describing.

Side note: Values are case sensitive so red is not the same as Red. This is the source of much frustration in conditional reporting.

## How and Where to Comment in Report Studio

Within any complex calculation or filter, you can (should) put comments into the code. The commenting syntax comes from a combination of Cognos Macros and C commenting style, but you can add comments explaining what you are intending with a specific part of Report Studio.

To enter a comment into Report Studio, you place a pair of pound signs (#) around a C-style block comment /*  Your Comment goes here */

So the whole thing looks like this

#/* this is the comment */#

Start your comment off with

#/* (pound, forward slash, asterisk)

End your Comments with

*/# ( asterisk, forward slash, pound)

(The set of characters are symmetrical)

I advise you to add comments in every filter and data item where you refer to anything other than a field (calculation, in-column filter or parameter reference)

A bonus for filter commenting is, that if you put the comment as the top line of the filter, Your comment will be readable in the filters list so you can identify them by name and not have to open several in order to find the one you are interested in.

# Parameters Cannot be Used in Conditional Expressions What to Do?

I don't really know why, but it's been this way for a long time in Report Studio, but you can't directly use a parameter in a conditional expression.

A common use of a parameter in a conditional expression could for instance turn part of the report red based on a value supplied by the end user at run time within the conditional expression.

As a developer, when I first learned Report Studio, I tried to use the parameter name directly in the conditional expression but got an error. In effect, I was trying to use the parameter as a programmer would use a global value...something that has its value set once and is available everywhere.

## How to Use Parameters in Conditional Expressions

To use parameters in conditional expressions, first take the parameter and drive it into your query so that the parameter value is available as a field value, THEN you can use the user entered value in a conditional expression and continue building your report as intended.

To do this you merely open your query, and drag a data item in from the toolbox. Then when you are writing the expression for the data item, you go to the fifth (parameters) tab under the insertable objects and drag in your parameter. Your data item should look something like this:

```
?pProduct?
```

Test it by viewing the tabular data of the same query, answering the prompt and verifying the prompt value ends up in every row of the query.

Alternatively, if you wish, you could perform the same logic that you intended to place within the conditional expression in the data item. Doing this would simplify your conditional expression. Also, moving the logic into your data item can possibly impact your performance in a positive way so it is worth trying.

Once it is in the query, you can use it as any other field in the conditional expression and proceed as normal.

# Techniques for Testing Queries

You are strongly advised that you test your queries individually as you go and find any problems and fix them as you find them. Doing so later is exponentially more difficult. You should even test one query as you add new fields and filters to make sure you are getting the right results and that problems are not occurring. You do not need to test as you add each field but do so every 4-5, every time you add a filter, add a calculation or perform a join or union.

## View Tabular Data

This menu option allows you to run one individual query and see the result set as a list report. There are several places where you can run the View Tabular data feature... You can do it from the run menu, you can also do it by right clicking on the image of a query. Finally, when an individual query is open (you are seeing the field definition) you can right click the explorer bar and see view tabular data in the window.

When you do perform a view tabular data, Report Studio will always warn you with a dialog box. You can just click the warning as it almost never is a concern to you.

To illustrate the usefulness of View Tabular Data, imagine that you are building a join in order to fulfill a report requirement. You have one base query and one lookup query executing and the final (joined) query attached to the report frame. But something is wrong.

First, navigate to the queries screen where you see all queries listed, right click the first base query of the set, and choose “view tabular data”. Review the data to make sure it contains what you were expecting. If that seems OK, do the same with the second query (the underlying query) and take a look at the data there. Finally, do the same with the Final query (the result of the joined query) and take a look. Almost certainly you will discover your problem if you are looking carefully at your data. You will repeat this technique hundreds of times and it is the core of my troubleshooting process.

## Turning Off Auto Group and Summary

Recall that Report Studio reports are aggregated based on the unique combination of values in fields in the report by default. It is common that there are problems in your data at a level that is below the lowest level in the report, but since aggregation is occurring, you only will see wrong values in your report and not have any visibility into why. Temporarily turning off auto aggregation is the solution here.

Auto group and summary is the first property of a query. To see the properties of a Query, you need to select a Query (single click) from the screen where you see all queries. Once you turn off the auto group and summary, you will see every record in the query. Take a look at your data.

For example: Your report shows the total unit sales by product for one day in a store. You sell 3 different products, but comparing your report to the sales receipts, you feel something is wrong. Product "C" seems too high.

| Product | Units Sold |
| --- | --- |
| A | 2 |
| B | 4 |
| B | 35 |

You turn off auto group and summary you see:

| Product | Units Sold |
|---|---|
| A | 1 |
| A | 1 |
| B | 1 |
| B | 2 |
| B | 1 |
| C | 1 |
| C | 33 |
| C | 1 |

The second to last line clearly seems to have a problem. Perhaps the system used to enter the quantity has a problem, or the clerk was not paying attention but what should have been 3 was entered as 33.

This is the type of thing that turning off the auto group and summarize property can uncover for you. The solution may sometimes be difficult and out of your area of understanding or responsibility, but this is part of making accurate reports. You frequently need to get to the bottom of data problems whether or not you caused them.

What you are typically looking for is repeating data that you did not expect to see, blank or null values that could change your calculations, negative values where you only expected to find positive values, weird dates, numbers way out of typical range, wrong values in fields (like a persons' name in a city field) and in general, any data that you did not expect to see.

## What is the Solution Based on your Findings?

This can go in many different ways. You could have a modeling problem causing unintended repeating of values. The model may be using the wrong join showing you records you do not expect to see or not seeing ones you do expect to see. You could be learning about the true nature of your data and may need to do additional filtering, calculations or summary functions. You may have an error in your query joins causing you to get (or drop) unexpected data. The fields you use in the two queries of the joins many have data that is not matching. The key here is to look and think about what you are seeing and to think through how Cognos will treat the data based on your understanding of aggregation, calculations, filters, joins, unions, etc...

The most common outcome is that you learn something about your data. It is very common that the data is not as clean as you would expect. There are many causes of bad data: Application bugs, application improvements over time, bad database architecture, changing business rules, DBA mistakes and more all impact data quality, especially over longer periods of time. Records of sales that happened in the past but future dates were entered, negative quantities ordered, towns in the wrong states, and pretty much anything that you could imagine can and does regularly appear in the data.

It is a reality of the report building job that you will have to deal with dirty data. As a report developer, you will frequently be putting in filters to eliminate bad data from your reports or calculations to fix deficient data. You may also be called upon to make reports to find bad data as part of a data cleanup effort.

## Remember to Turn Auto Group & Summary Back On

The most important thing here is to remember that you have turned auto summarization off, as later you will typically want to turn it back on. It's a property that is infrequently used for reporting, but more so for troubleshooting. If you forget to turn it off, the symptom you will see is your report will have much more data and you will see duplicated values in your text columns where before, you saw only unique combinations.

# Using Logic Within Filters

Within filter expressions, you can use “if “and other logical instructions. The usefulness of this is often not intuitive, but it will enable you to do some things that are either time saving, or capability expanding.

Perhaps the most important thing you can do with this technique is control whether or not to apply a filter based on the answer to a prompt.

In this scenario, you create a prompt with static set of choices then use the result of the users’ choice in your filter expression to determine which filter to apply.

For example, say you have a database table where rows are not deleted from the table, but instead you have a field indicating whether or not the record is deleted. Your report may normally need to exclude deleted records, but you may have a report requirement that allows the user to see only deleted rows, both deleted and non-deleted, or just non-deleted. In this case, you could make a radio button group prompt with 3 values. The parameter for the prompt should then be used in the filter expression, in either an if/else if block or even a case statement. So something like:

```
if (?pFilter?=’deleted’) then
  ([mypackage].[table1].[deleted]=true)
else if (?pFilter?=’nondeleted’) then
  ([mypackage].[table1].[deleted]=false)
else
  (1=1)
end
```

So using the logic above you are specifying a different filter based on the answer to the prompt where the actual logic of the filter is specified within the if structure.

An interesting thing to note from above is the final condition. It turns out that you always need something in your expression within the filter code, so the logic above (1=1) is sent to the database and returns all records... in effect no filter is applied.

Here's another scenario to help you understand the usefulness.

Imagine you have a food business where each day of the week, you have a special sale of the day and, in your report, you want to omit the sales from your special from your other sales. You could write a logical expression to filter out Monday's special when today is Monday, Tuesday's special on Tuesday etc.

# Build Complex Calculations as a Series of Smaller Calculations (Bonus Tip #11)

Some calculations you will write can have numerous fields with multiple sets of parenthesis as well as math operations and function calls. If you try to write the entire calculation into one data item, troubleshooting the calculation could be extremely difficult and frustrating.

The trick here is to not write a big calculation into one data item, but instead break the calculation into a series of smaller sub-calculations that are later brought together in other data items to construct your final value.

Having the individual pieces makes finding what is wrong much easier.

This technique may come at the cost of a small performance hit, but once you have the parts working, you can later combine them back into one calculation. If you do, I recommend that you do not remove the components, but instead comment them out. Should you later discover you have a problem, you can easily uncomment them and begin your debugging.

## My Technique for Debugging Calculations:

To make sure my calculations are working, I will take a sample of raw data from the database directly and bring it into Excel. Then, adding individual additional columns in Excel, perform the same parts of the calculation that you have done in your Report Studio query. Comparing your spreadsheet columns to the View Tabular Data of the same set of data will show you which step in your calculation is in error. If both match and are both wrong, the problem is in your understanding of the calculation or in the data. Misplaced parenthesis are among the most common mistake you will make.

One other thing you can do to help you focus on the problem is to add some temporary filters to the report in order to focus on a small set of data during debugging and the delete the filter once you have fixed the problem. During your development, make sure to later modify your filter to see a larger sample of data as you may have chosen a sample that does not contain issues that impact your results.

# Conclusion

Knowing how to use a tool is merely the start of being a developer in any technology. Report Studio is no different.

These tips are designed to make you more productive today and going forward. You can now solve your problems in more creative ways that you hopefully knew before.

Understanding these eleven tips about creating reports will go a long way toward helping you approach development problems in a more evolved way. Instead of just beginning to build a report, you should now be able to take time to disassemble a report specification, devise a strategy for creating the proper report structure and then implement it.

For example, you now should understand that if you have to show data on the same row which has different filter conditions, you know you will need multiple queries and joins to solve it or may consider using an in-column filter.

The first step always in my debugging is to look at the data produced by the queries. Using View Tabular Data and turning off auto group and summarize are two tips that will do wonders for your speed of debugging and enhancement of your understanding of your data so crucial to report development.

Adding comments to your reports is not intuitive or even close to any standard from any development technology and now you can do it for filters and calculations helping the understandability and internal documentation of your reports.

I have intentionally made much of this material very concise and reduced it to the simplest way of saying it. Please do not take its length as an indication of relative importance. Some things I say in one sentence have taken me years of hands on experience to write.

Re-read this booklet (or one section) from time to time and you will continue to gain a deeper understanding of how Report Studio wants to be used. I hope you agree that the "what you should do" is rarely taught but instead learned, and learned the hard way, and it is my sincere hope that I have brought you some of the “what you should do”.

# About the Author

Ray Hogan is a 30 year hands on diverse technologist. He has spent the bulk of his career as an applications developer working on Relational Database applications. He has learned and subsequently discarded technologies many times with the changing nature of IT.

Ray has an unusual combination of skills in that he can both do technology and teach technology. On top of his 28 years of teaching experience (karate), He spent 2, 3 year periods as a technical trainer teaching Web Development in the late 90's and then for Cognos as a Trainer in the mid 00's. As a trainer, he has a knack for simplifying complex things, providing multiple descriptions of the same thing and caring that his students succeed. As a developer, he believes that simplicity is better but simplicity is not necessarily easy. He also believes that underlying principles will help you

He currently is a VP of Business Intelligence doing hands on report development, training and software development at a Major Financial Institution in the NYC area.

He is certified in Cognos (reporting, modeling and administration), and is a Certified Technical Trainer (CTT+). He has a B.S. in Electronics Engineering and is pursuing a Masters in Information Systems.

You can find Ray at CognosTrainers.com, and on LinkedIn.

# Services and Products

## Cognos Training

We provide in-class and virtual, hands-on training in all parts of Cognos. We distinguish ourselves in that our trainers have significant development experience and are excellent trainers. At the core of our trainer selection is the observation that just because a person has a technical skill, does not mean they can teach it. We use only trainers who have very significant development experience AND can explain the tools in an understandable way to people of differing technical backgrounds.

The value of a great trainer cannot be understated. Lesser trainers focus on what a feature does ... we focus on what it does for you, when to use it, alternatives and other value-creating instruction. In short, we teach you what you should do, not what you can do. We want our students to get it, to experience several "ah-has'" in our classes. We can provide training using your data. This greatly helps students understand the tools as they understand the answers they are receiving within they reports and can better grasp the cause and effect so crucial to effective training. Moreover, students leave the training much more prepared to build reports against your data. Training can be on your equipment or ours. We can provide any subset or combination of classes as you need.

**Our rates are highly competitive.**

**Onsite or virtual. One hour or one month.**

## JavaScript Report Enhancement

It is pretty common that you need Report Studio prompts to do more than they are designed to do. Enforcing data entry rules like data type, number of choices, date restrictions and more are not possible out of the box. Additionally, there are some things the Report Studio prompts cannot do like synchronizing choices between different prompts, taking a pasted list of values as a filter condition, and other higher level prompt actions.  In short, you can get more out of Report Studio by using JavaScript. You can even do some report side enhancements like animated chart rotation, showing additional data in hover-overs, Ajax and more.

Finding someone with both Report Studio development experience and JavaScript programming skills is very difficult. Sure there are those who can copy and paste from Google, but often, you need even more.

If you need to enhance your prompts or reports with JavaScript, We know how to do it and have an extensive library of routines. The typical JavaScript assignment takes 4 hours or less. See our website for videos of some fairly advanced Report Studio prompt enhancements we have made.

## Consulting

Tell us how we can help you. We can act as a Sounding Board, Brainstorming, Report Troubleshooting, Build Report Conversion tools, Candidate Interviewing, extremely specific (single topic) training.... How can we help you?

## Other Booklets

Our Companion Book is "Ten Core Principles of Report Studio Development" covers specific techniques and other things you can do to increase your development skills. Stay in touch for Additional Report Studio Series booklets coming soon. We'll be announcing them to LinkedIn and through our email list.

Made in the USA
Monee, IL
04 November 2026

67384419R00026